Spelling Today

for ages 9-10

...includes words, spelling patterns and spelling rules recommended for Year 5 pupils.

How to use this book:

1. Look at the rules and words featured on the right-hand pages.
2. Turn over the page to look at each word on the left-hand page.
3. Cover the word with the flap, then write the word.
4. Uncover the word to check that you haven't made a mistake.
5. Write the word again for extra practice.

Singular and plural words

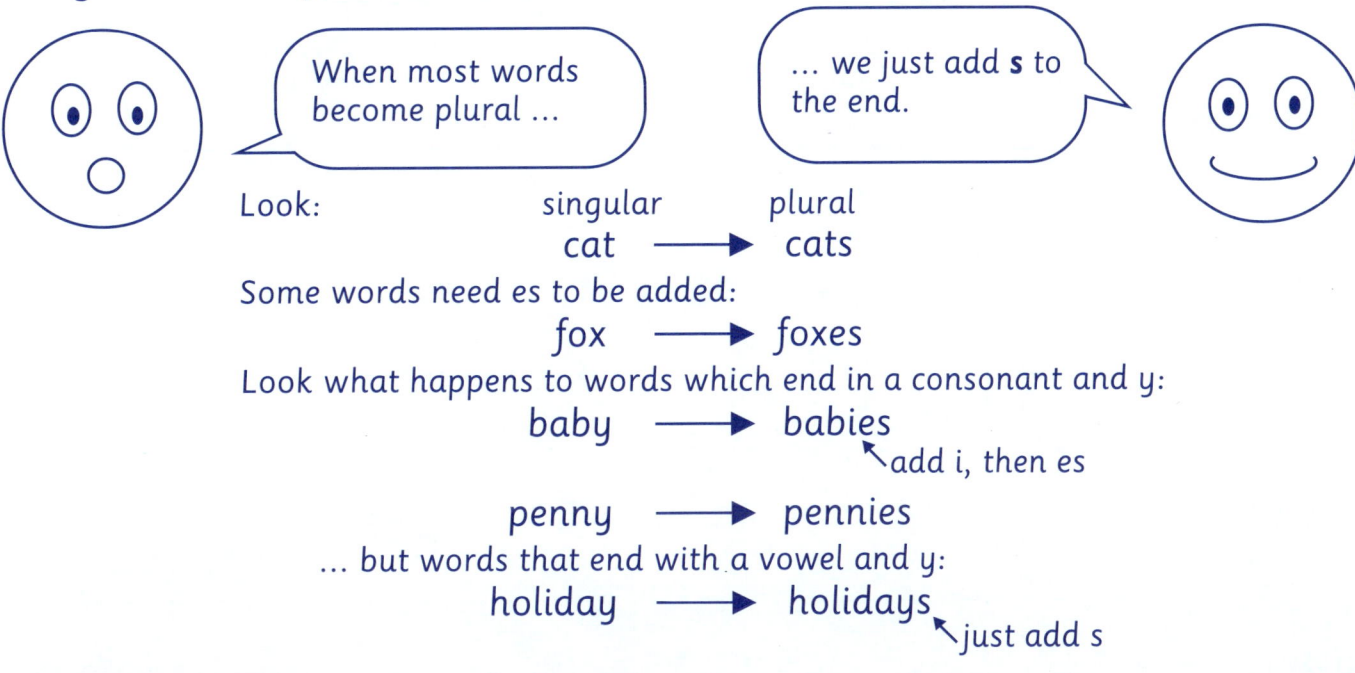

When most words become plural ... ... we just add **s** to the end.

Look:　　　　　singular　　　plural
　　　　　　　　cat ⟶ cats

Some words need es to be added:
　　　　　　　　fox ⟶ foxes

Look what happens to words which end in a consonant and y:
　　　　　　　　baby ⟶ babies
　　　　　　　　　　　　　add i, then es

　　　　　　　　penny ⟶ pennies

... but words that end with a vowel and y:
　　　　　　　　holiday ⟶ holidays
　　　　　　　　　　　　　　just add s

Write the plural words for the singular words listed:

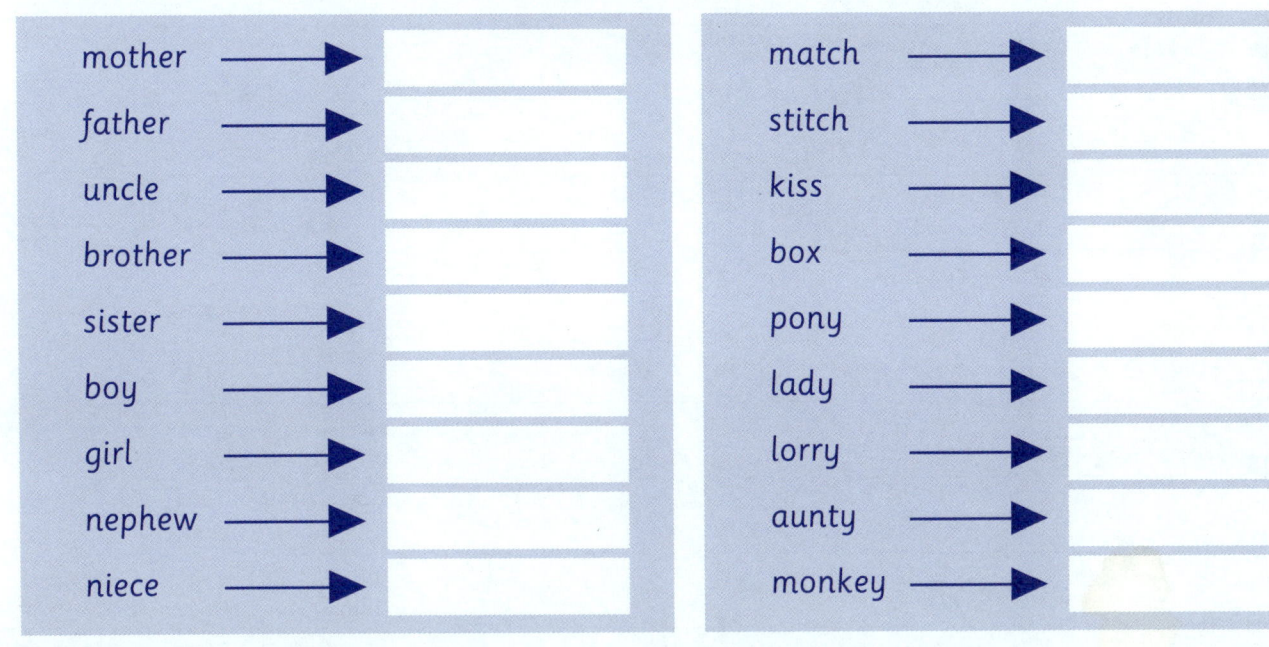

mother ⟶		match ⟶	
father ⟶		stitch ⟶	
uncle ⟶		kiss ⟶	
brother ⟶		box ⟶	
sister ⟶		pony ⟶	
boy ⟶		lady ⟶	
girl ⟶		lorry ⟶	
nephew ⟶		aunty ⟶	
niece ⟶		monkey ⟶	

Step 1
Look and learn, then cover the word with the flap.

Step 2
Write the word, then see if it's correct.

Step 3
Write the word again. Say it as you write it.

uncles

aunties

nephews

nieces

parents

adults

kisses

babies

stitches

boxes

ladies

lorries

monkeys

trolleys

displays

holidays

Singular words which end in vowels other than e

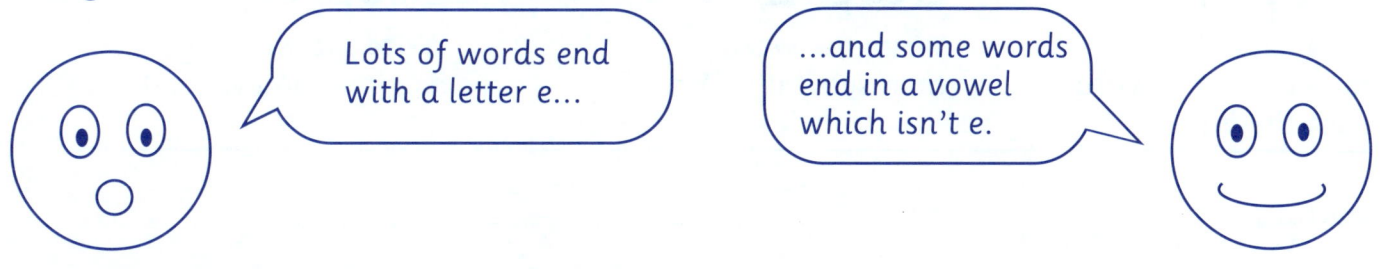

Lots of words end with a letter e...

...and some words end in a vowel which isn't e.

Make these words into plurals just by adding s:

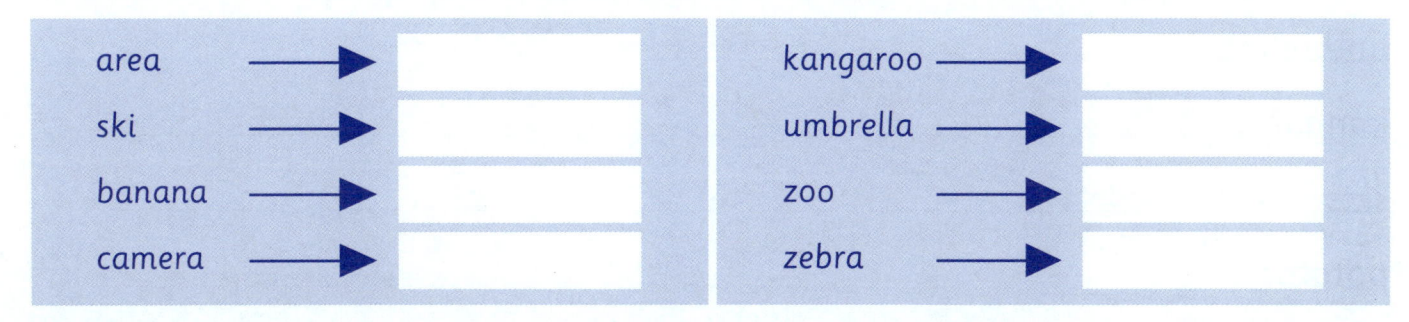

area →		kangaroo →	
ski →		umbrella →	
banana →		zoo →	
camera →		zebra →	

Words which end with a consonant then o usually need es to make them plural:

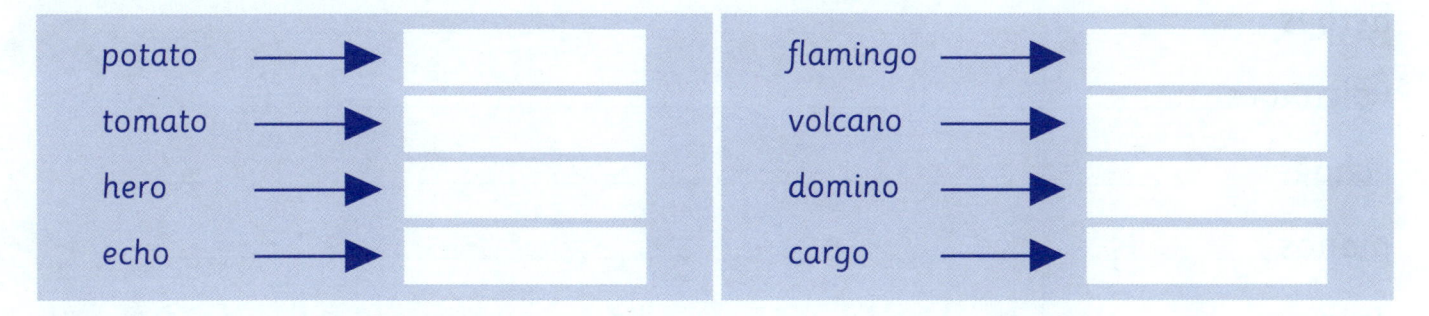

potato →		flamingo →	
tomato →		volcano →	
hero →		domino →	
echo →		cargo →	

...but some words which end with the letter o just need s to be added:

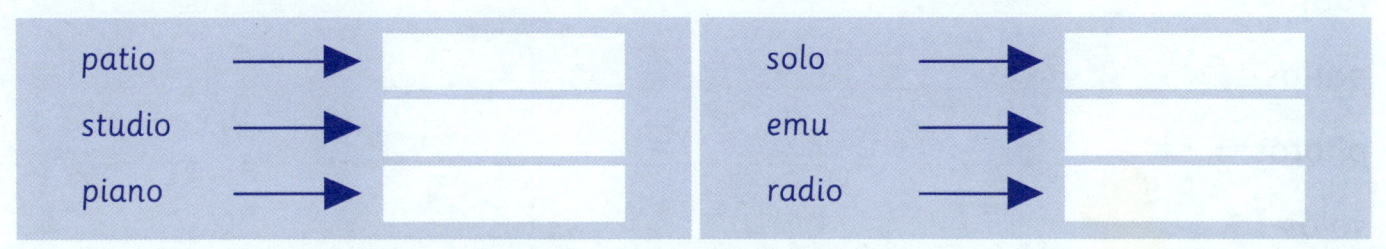

patio →		solo →	
studio →		emu →	
piano →		radio →	

Step 1
Look and learn, then cover the word with the flap.

Step 2
Write the word, then see if it's correct.

Step 3
Write the word again. Say it as you write it.

bananas		
cameras		
umbrellas		
kangaroos		
skis		
potatoes		
tomatoes		
heroes		
volcanoes		
echoes		
pianos		
studios		
radios		
patios		
photos		
solos		

Strange plurals

*Words which end with **fe** or a single letter **f** ...*

*... usually have to lose the letter **f** and have **ves** added to make them plural.*

Everyone had to run for their _____ when a pack of _____ attacked the village.

The _____ came to the farm and stole the _____ .

I bought three _____ of bread, then I cut each one into two _____ using one of the sharp kitchen _____ .

Tarun put all the books back on the _____ .

word-bank

wolf → wolves   thief → thieves
loaf → loaves   knife → knives   half → halves
shelf → shelves   calf → calves   life → lives

Find the plural for each singular word:

fungus → _____   tooth → _____

mouse → _____   foot → _____

child → _____   goose → _____

woman → _____   sheep → _____

word-bank
feet   children   mice   geese   women   sheep   fungi   teeth

7

Step 1
Look and learn, then cover the word with the flap.

Step 2
Write the word, then see if it's correct.

Step 3
Write the word again. Say it as you write it.

woman

women

goose

geese

leaf

leaves

knife

knives

children

thief

thieves

half

halves

fungus

fungi

shelves

Useful words

Use the words from the word-bank... ...to fill the gaps in the story.

Yesterday my little _____ had his _____ party. He wanted to go swimming but Mum said he couldn't because the _____ might fall in! We had the party in our back _____ and lots of _____ came. They each brought _____ for my brother.

Everybody had a _____ time. One boy said that our garden was the best place in the _____ because there was so much mud and he liked getting his _____ dirty! I didn't think his mum would be very _____ because of having to wash his clothes!

I was _____ that the children had a nice time until I _____ one girl say that her _____ was hurting. My mum had a quiet _____ with her and gave her a _____ to cheer her up. It seemed to _____.

word-bank

head   sure   great   swimming   garden
birthday   baby   work   heard   world   brother
clothes   children   happy   balloon   those   something   word

Step 1
Look and learn, then cover the word with the flap.

Step 2
Write the word, then see if it's correct.

Step 3
Write the word again. Say it as you write it.

swimming		
those		
birthday		
world		
work		
word		
head		
heard		
children		
baby		
brother		
happy		
garden		
sure		
something		
clothes		

Word families

Sort the words in the word-bank ...

... so that they are in word families.

word-bank

electric   action   recover   public   delight
light   assist   cover   delighted
actor   examine   electrician   activity   examination   discover   assistant
publication   electronic   react   uncover   assistance   publicity
electrical   reaction   electricity   publish   act   lightning   examiner

cover

act

public

electric

examine

light

assist

11

Step 1
Look and learn, then cover the word with the flap.

Step 2
Write the word, then see if it's correct.

Step 3
Write the word again. Say it as you write it.

electric

electricity

light

lightning

lighten

delight

examine

examination

recover

recovery

action

activity

public

publication

assist

assistant

More word families

"Sort the words in the word-bank …"

"… so that they are in word families."

word-bank

improve circulate medical operator
related approve circular disapprove
cooperate medic improvement relative circulation unrelated
operation medication prove operate circle approval
relation relate cooperation medicine disapproval

circle

prove

medic

operate

relate

Step 1
Look and learn, then cover the word with the flap.

Step 2
Write the word, then see if it's correct.

Step 3
Write the word again. Say it as you write it.

medicine

medical

operate

operation

operator

prove

improve

improvement

disapprove

related

relation

relative

circle

circular

circulation

circulate

Adding full, till or all to other word parts

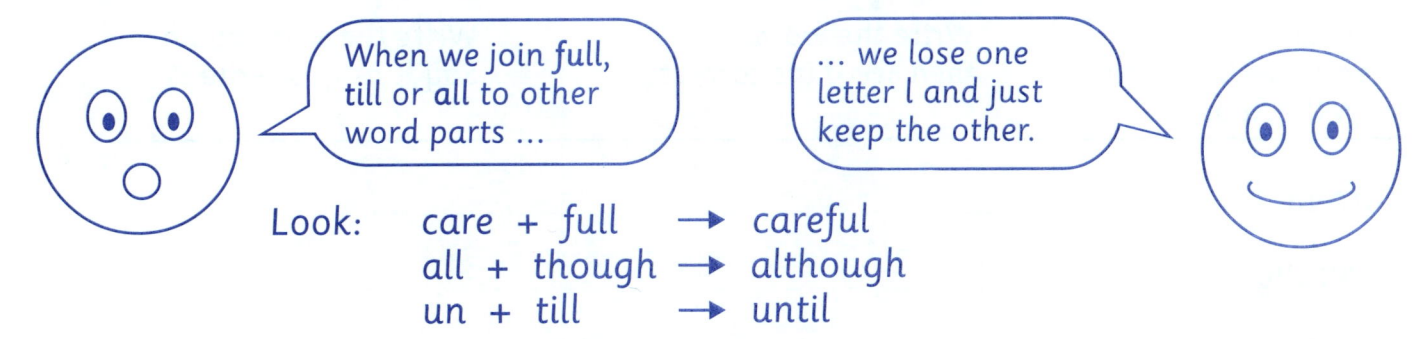

When we join full, till or all to other word parts ...

... we lose one letter l and just keep the other.

Look: care + full → careful
        all + though → although
        un + till → until

... but notice what happens when we add ly to the words ending in ful:

care + full → careful + ly → carefully

Fill the gaps in this table:

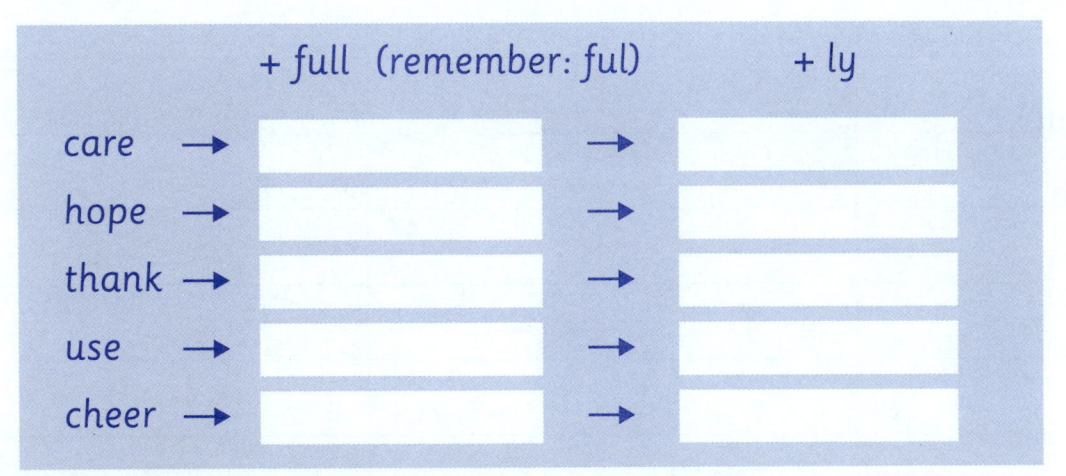

	+ full (remember: ful)	+ ly
care →		
hope →		
thank →		
use →		
cheer →		

What happens to the word beauty?

beauty + full → beautiful + ly → beautifully

Look at these words:

all + ways → always   well + come → welcome

15

Step 1
Look and learn, then cover the word with the flap.

Step 2
Write the word, then see if it's correct.

Step 3
Write the word again. Say it as you write it.

careful		
carefully		
hopeful		
hopefully		
useful		
usefully		
cheerful		
cheerfully		
although		
almost		
always		
already		
welcome		
skill		
skilful		
skilfully		

Adding ing

Look carefully at the rules for adding ing.

For example, if a word ends with a consonant, with a vowel in front of it, we need to double the consonant.

1. Words ending with a single vowel and a single consonant: for example, **sit**:

    sit + ing → sitting
    double the consonant

2. Words ending with two (or more) consonants: for example, **camp**:

    camp + ing → camping
    just add ing

3. Words ending with two vowels before a single consonant: for example, **sleep**:

    sleep + ing → sleeping
    just add ing

4. Words ending with an e: for example, **write**:

    write + ing → writing
    take off the e, then add ing

5. Words ending with a letter y: for example, **hurry**:

    hurry + ing → hurrying
    just add ing

Use the rules to add ing to these words:

shop →	stop →	grin →
burst →	park →	comb →
sweep →	float →	buy →
hope →	come →	make →

Step 1
Look and learn, then cover the word with the flap.

Step 2
Write the word, then see if it's correct.

Step 3
Write the word again. Say it as you write it.

hurrying

writing

shopping

stopping

drumming

counting

parking

combing

sweeping

floating

shouting

hoping

coming

making

calling

falling

Words ending with letter e

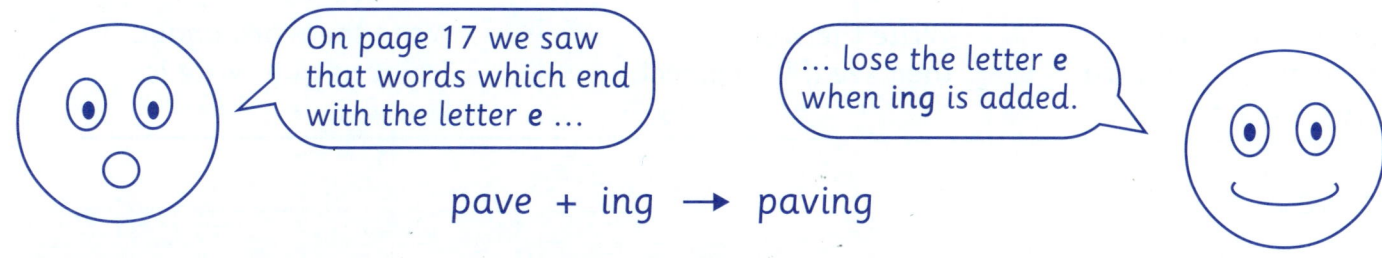

On page 17 we saw that words which end with the letter e ...

... lose the letter e when ing is added.

pave + ing → paving

Look what happens when we add other suffixes:

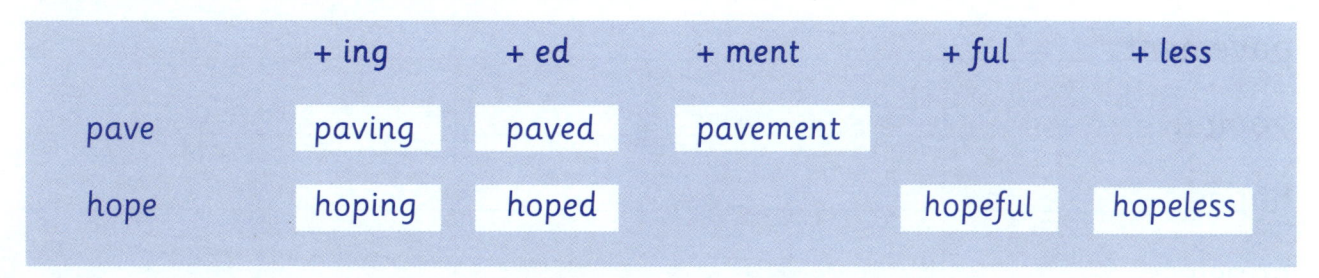

	+ ing	+ ed	+ ment	+ ful	+ less
pave	paving	paved	pavement		
hope	hoping	hoped		hopeful	hopeless

Fill the gaps in this chart:

	+ ing	+ ed	+ ful	+ less
care				
use				
tune				
glue				
resource				
whine				
slope				
shame				

| Step 1
Look and learn, then cover the word with the flap. | Step 2
Write the word, then see if it's correct. | Step 3
Write the word again. Say it as you write it. |
---|---|---
pave | |
paving | |
pavement | |
hoping | |
hoped | |
hopeless | |
come | |
coming | |
using | |
useful | |
useless | |
whine | |
whining | |
whined | |
resourceful | |
shameless | |

Hard c and soft c

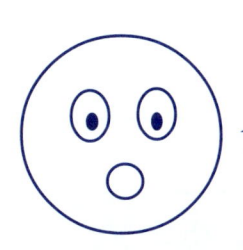

Sometimes the letter **c** has a hard sound, as in **camera**.

Sometimes the letter **c** has a soft sound, as in **centimetre**.

word-bank

calendar   certain   cylinder   calculator   December   cat   curtains   cinema   century   dance   recent   carriage   city   camera   coat   coming   centre   cupboard   disco   pencil   computer   carried   notice   palace

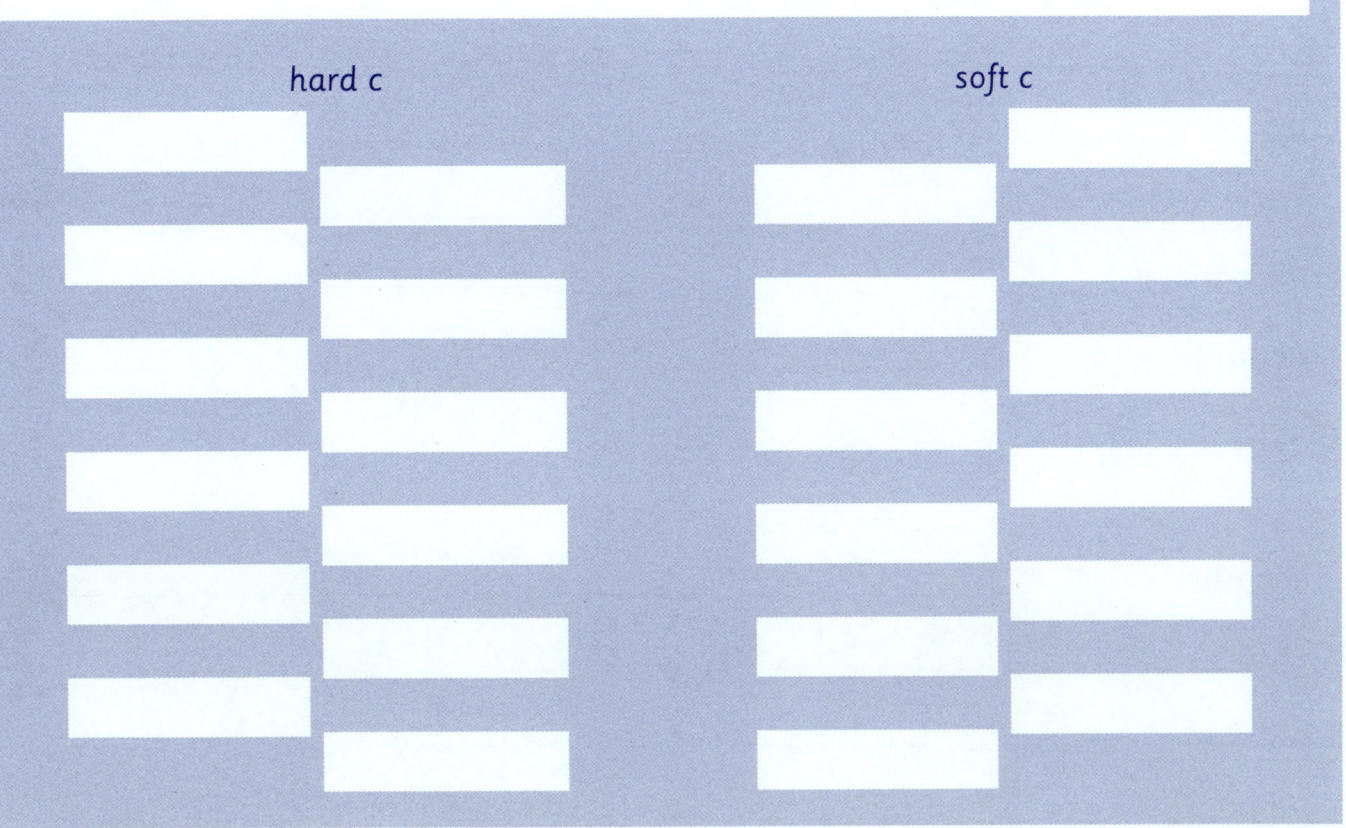

hard c

soft c

Step 1
Look and learn, then cover the word with the flap.

Step 2
Write the word, then see if it's correct.

Step 3
Write the word again. Say it as you write it.

city

cities

camera

calculator

dance

disco

coat

centre

cupboard

calendar

recent

recently

December

October

calling

cinema

Use the words from the word-bank...

...to fill the gaps in the story.

Yesterday was a very _____ day. My little _____ Lucy went with my _____ and _____ to have her eyes tested. She had to sit on a special high chair because she's so _____. She had to read some big _____ letters on a _____ paper background. Then the _____ shone a bright _____ into her _____. Mum said that Lucy didn't make a _____. She was very quiet the _____ time they were in the opticians. She couldn't understand _____ they were in there.

When they came out she just wanted to spend her pocket _____. Dad said she looked in the _____ of each shop they passed. They tried to find something that didn't cost the _____. Lucy said that her _____ had bead bracelets and she wanted one of her _____.

word-bank

important, sister, sound, small, white, paper, black, whole, window, earth, own, light, why, friends, lady, eyes, father, mother, money

Step 1
Look and learn, then cover the word with the flap.

Step 2
Write the word, then see if it's correct.

Step 3
Write the word again. Say it as you write it.

mother

father

sister

lady

friends

earth

eyes

important

sound

paper

black

white

whole

money

window

light

More word families

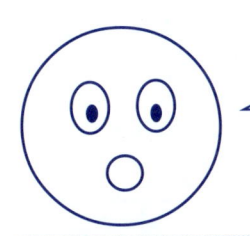

Sort the words in the word-bank ...

... so that they are in word families.

word-bank

cough thief colour eight learn
mood tight piece favour
enough year cookery frighten frightening bought friend
hour goodness earth book height brought field
favourite wear neighbours thoughtful

ie

oo

ear

ough

ight

our

Step 1
Look and learn, then cover the word with the flap.

Step 2
Write the word, then see if it's correct.

Step 3
Write the word again. Say it as you write it.

football

moody

weight

right

heart

heard

nearly

clearly

tried

cried

pieces

thought

through

flavour

favourite

colourful

Homophones

Homophones are words which sound the same...

...but which mean different things.

Choose the correct word to fill each gap:

waist / waste	She thought that the skirt was a _____ of material because it went round her _____ twice.
board / bored	I was very _____ when the teacher was writing on the _____ .
peace / piece	Mum had a _____ of cake while there was some _____ and quiet.
him / hymn	The headteacher asked _____ to play a _____ on his recorder.
aloud / allowed	When we had a maths test we were not _____ to talk _____ .
cereal / serial	He ate his breakfast _____ while he watched the _____ on the television.
seen / scene	She says she has _____ the play, 'Macbeth'. The first _____ features some witches.
knight / night	Last _____ I dreamt that a _____ rode past on his horse.
break / brake	During his lunch _____ he tested the front _____ on his bike.
key / quay	I lost the car _____ when I was down at the _____ looking at the boats.

27

Step 1
Look and learn, then cover the word with the flap.

Step 2
Write the word, then see if it's correct.

Step 3
Write the word again. Say it as you write it.

cereals

serial

quay

scene

peace

hymn

knight

night

break

brakes

waist

waste

aloud

allowed

board

bored

Suffixes: tion

"Several endings make the **tion** (shun) sound …"

"… but **t i o n** is the most common spelling."

Sort the words into word families:

word-bank

concentration   completion   evolution
description   exception   addition   fiction
mention   suggestion   lotion   action   attention   expedition   station
reception   question   invitation   emotion   pollution   position

…ation

…ition

…ption

…ction

…ntion

…stion

…etion

…otion

…ution

29

Step 1
Look and learn, then cover the word with the flap.

Step 2
Write the word, then see if it's correct.

Step 3
Write the word again. Say it as you write it.

concentration

invitation

relation

fiction

fraction

competition

addition

expedition

position

condition

potion

promotion

description

mention

question

solution

Suffixes: sion

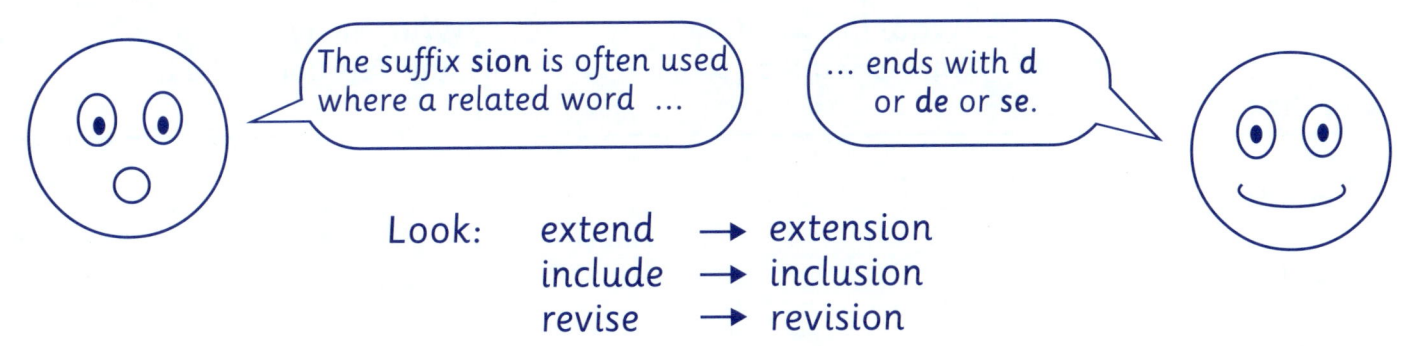

"The suffix **sion** is often used where a related word ..."

"... ends with **d** or **de** or **se**."

Look: extend → extension
include → inclusion
revise → revision

Change these words to **sion** words:

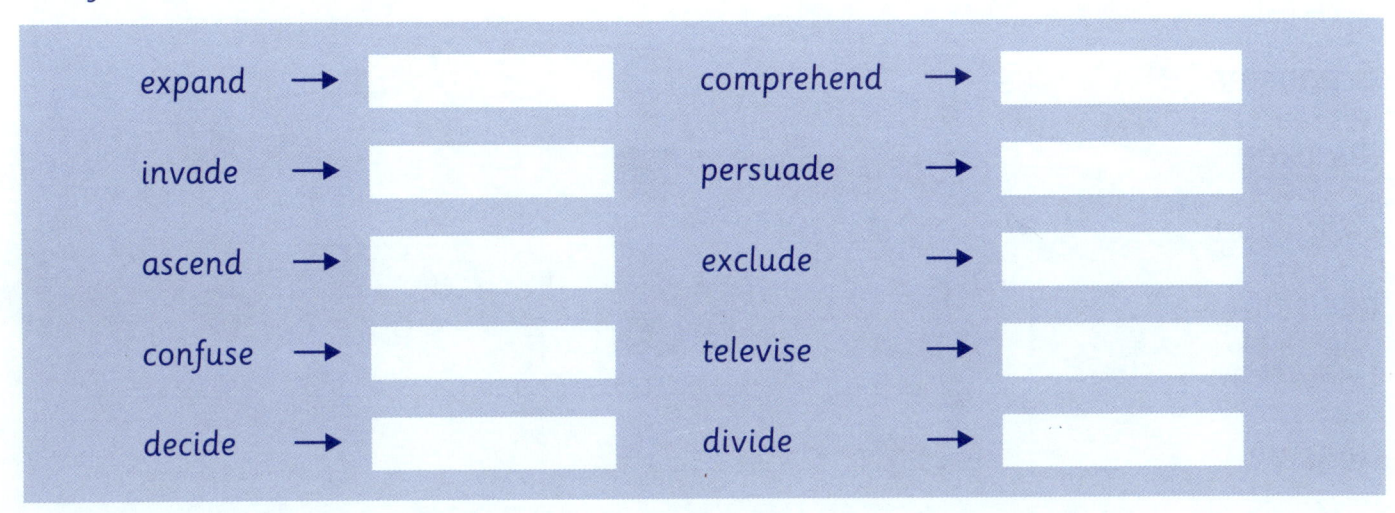

expand →		comprehend →	
invade →		persuade →	
ascend →		exclude →	
confuse →		televise →	
decide →		divide →	

Practise these **ssion** words:

admission

discussion

expression

impression

permission

profession

Step 1
Look and learn, then cover the word with the flap.

Step 2
Write the word, then see if it's correct.

Step 3
Write the word again. Say it as you write it.

extension

inclusion

exclusion

revision

expansion

invasion

confusion

decision

television

division

collision

conclusion

occasion

mission

permission

possession

cian, tian, sian, cean

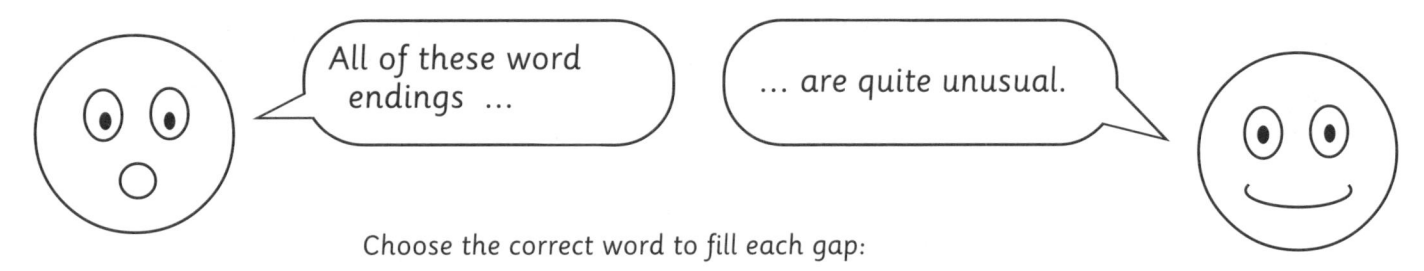

All of these word endings ...

... are quite unusual.

Choose the correct word to fill each gap:

politician	An _____	examines people's eyes.
optician	A _____	performs tricks.
electrician	A _____	works in politics.
magician	An _____	repairs wiring.
musician	A _____	plays an instrument.
Dalmatian	Some people think that _____ live on Mars.	
Alsatian	_____ people celebrate at Christmas.	
Christian	A _____ has lots of spots.	
Martians	An _____ is a large dog, with pointed ears.	

Practise these words:

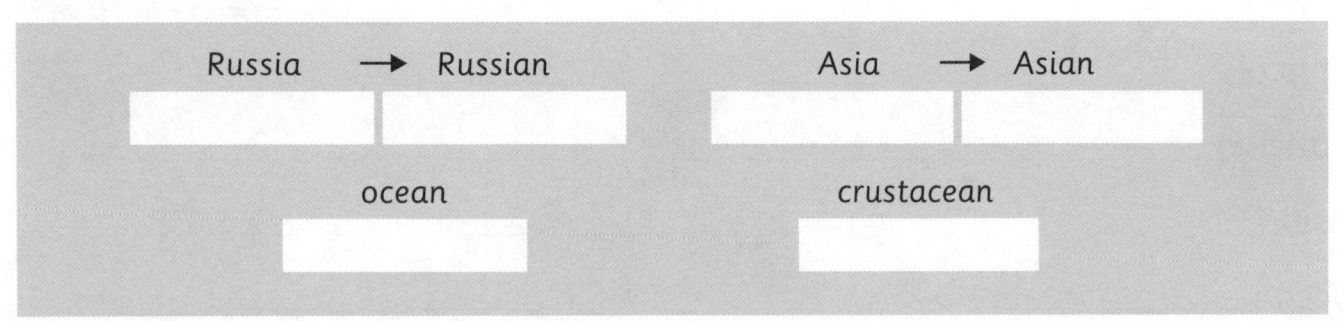

Russia → Russian   _____ _____

Asia → Asian   _____ _____

ocean   _____

crustacean   _____

33

Step 1
Look and learn, then cover the word with the flap.

Step 2
Write the word, then see if it's correct.

Step 3
Write the word again. Say it as you write it.

politics

political

politician

electric

electrical

electrician

magic

magical

magician

music

musical

musician

optical

optician

Asian

ocean

Lots of prefixes: **anti, de, dis, il, im, in, ir, pro, sus** and **un**

Practise these words with prefixes:

antifreeze		defrost	
antiseptic		depart	
anticlockwise		disadvantage	

legal → illegal		logical → illogical	
patient → impatient		possible → impossible	
sincere → insincere		direct → indirect	
regular → irregular		rational → irrational	

produce		profession	
producer		professional	
product		professor	
production		progress	
productive		progressing	
productivity		progression	

suspect		unlikely	
suspicion		unnecessary	
suspend		unreasonable	
suspension		unusual	

| Step 1
Look and learn, then cover the word with the flap. | Step 2
Write the word, then see if it's correct. | Step 3
Write the word again. Say it as you write it. |
|---|---|---|
| anticlockwise | | |
| departure | | |
| disadvantage | | |
| illegal | | |
| impatient | | |
| indirect | | |
| irregular | | |
| produce | | |
| production | | |
| profession | | |
| progress | | |
| suspect | | |
| suspension | | |
| unnecessary | | |
| unreasonable | | |
| unusual | | |